Broken Axle Spinning Blind
poetry from heart to mind

Acknowledgements

Thank you to my dear husband and children, for all your love and support.
Thank you to J. Nichole Noël for giving me the courage to realize a long held dream.

© 2010 by PRAS Publishing
All rights reserved under International and
Pan-American Copyright Conventions

Published in Toronto, Canada by
PRAS Publishing
www.pras.ca

Broken Axle Spinning Blind: Poetry from heart to mind
Written by Freyda Tartak
Cover design by Yevgenia Casale

For any requests regarding use of all or portions of this work
or how to order additional copies
email consult@pras.ca

Library and Archives Canada Cataloguing in Publication

Tartak, Freyda, 1973-
  Broken axle spinning blind : poetry from heart to mind / Freyda Tartak.

ISBN 978-0-9865142-0-3

  I. Title.

PS8639.A775B76 2010   C811'.6   C2010-900095-1

Broken Axle Spinning Blind
poetry from heart to mind

Freyda Tartak

PRAS *Publishing*
Toronto

This book is dedicated to my mother, for making it something worth reading, and to my father, for telling me I'm an engineer while teaching me how to be an artist.

~F.T.

Table of Contents

Fragment One: Emotions Dispersed 7
    For Love of Life 9
    Desire 10
    Attraction 11
    Suspicious Lover 12
    Dignity 13
    Anger 14
    Kiss Me 15
    Procrastination 16
    Regret 17
    Speechless 18
    Wrong Side of the Glass 19
    An Edited Excerpt from Tick Tock Tom 20
    Unsent Love Letter 21
    Past Midnight 22
    Love 23
    Should We? 24
    No Going Back 25
    Hollow Wishes 26

Piece Two: Introspection 29
    Cognac and Jasmine 31
    Mermaids' Song 32
    Aimless 34
    The Dove 35
    Some Guy on a Farm 36
    As Butterflies Dance 37
    Understand Me 38
    Breaking Away 39
    What Was Lost 40

 Sunrise 41
 Passing Through 42
 Now What? 43
 A Father's Love 44
 In Love We Repeat 45
 Rebirth 46
 Three Steps to Nowhere 47
 Doubt and Loathing 48
 Did You Ever? 49
 I want to start my day 50
 The ABCs of Captions 51

Shard Three: Life Lessons 53
 Losing at Love 55
 Boy Parts 56
 Dinosaurs 57
 Forest Stream 58
 Free of You 59
 Love Forgotten 60
 I Loved You in Silence 61
 He's Gone, Was It Worth It? 62
 Oh, Maryanne 63
 Oxymoron 64
 American Dollars 65
 Ruins of a Party 66
 Remnants of the Day 67

Hunk Four: Commitment 69
 Follow Along 71
 The Honeymoon 72
 Anticipation 73
 Never Apart 74
 All I want is 75

Making Amends	76
Besieged	77
Blood Thick Anger	78
Husband	79

Splinter Five: Innocence To Crush Or Mold 81

Listen to me	83
Toddler Trot	84
Teacher's Day	85
Voices	86
Baking Cookies	87
Growing Pains	88
Perpetual Motion	89
In Sickness	90
Halloween Dread	91
Big Eyes Round World	92
That face you make	93
Frustration	94
Sadness	95
The Fifth Sense	96

Sliver Six: The Sum and Its Parts 99

Tap, Tap, Tap	101
Chipmunks and Ground Squirrels	102
The Shore	103
Energy	104
Moonlight	105
Earth's Bones	106
Hush	107
Rocks & Stars	108
Quest for Satisfaction	109
A Dream Realized	110
Broken Axle Spinning Blind	111

A Soul Laid Bare 112
Missing the Bus 113
Afterword 115
Secret Passage 117
About The Author 129

Fragment One: Emotions Dispersed

For Love of Life

Love is possibility
Solitude is calm
Calm and gently breathing

New life gently stirring
Within and then without
There is no life without it
Existence in account

Without its gentle fire
Like air and love beneath
Like air it floats above me
Mistress hear my plea

Encompassing and bountiful
Without a vacuum stays
No breath or heartbeat pounding
In death at peace again

Desire

Of Gods and Queens and finer things
I do declare thee done

Of Kings, bar maids, and dust mites
My dreams are filled with none

Of suns and moons and silver slivers
I peak into new heights

Of love and lust and destiny
For you I do decline

Attraction

I love and fear you
Need you
Want you

In hindsight you'll rejoice
Your heart does not belong to me
But, you can stay and talk

A hollow thud followed his words
So, listen closely now
Your ears might wilt
If you reflect too closely

Feigned sighs be heard
His vows mean less than nothing
Accepting platitudes is fine
They lubricate the mind

If something isn't done tonight
There may still be some sunshine
Tomorrow to regret your deeds
Tonight is to unwind

Suspicious Lover

What's that she thought
A rash he said
Where did you go last night

Out with the boys
We got home late
You said you'd call
I waited by the phone

Why do those girls all know your name
Where did you leave your tie
Why do you think I'll buy your lies
Why do I let you make me cry

Dignity

It used to be that I could say
With merit and restraint
That when a breast of mine was shown
It would be with discretion

I used to care who saw it
It was for private view
This big round object of desire
That men were often drawn to

Nobody turns to look at me
As feeding time begins
We might be at the mall
We might be at the playground
We might be at a holy place
Or seated at the food court

Nobody cares to look my way
It does not shock or scare
Nobody thinks its odd to see
A boob in open daylight

One day I might just hide
This object of desire
That day is not today
My despot hankers for it

Anger

Encompassing and fascinating
Swallows you whole through your chest
Gathering heat at your cheek bones
Pushing steam through the pores on your face

Its scent evaporates off your shoulders
Muscles tightening below their blades
Runs down your spine to get to your tail bone
Wraps your hips like a lusty lover's hungry hands

The nails on its fingers rip through you
Flowing blood through your thighs, to your knees
The urge to move emancipates and engulfs you
Liberating the binds that keep you still

The cause racing and repeating through your head
Until it stops to matter
Slow down and stop
Grateful for a chance to get this self-engrossed

Deflated and alone surveying the surroundings
Remorse sets in as you quietly go home
Their trepidation at where you might have been
Replaced by gratitude for your return

Ire is the rain soon followed by a calm
Despite the tranquil silence there is private pleasure
A deep sigh in the shadow of burning emotion
Remains your secrete fortitude within

Kiss Me

Your kiss makes me want you
All reason suppressed
Numbness absorbs me
The sky a new hue

Unsure if you want me
My most basic urge
The blindest of curses
Too scared of what might never be

Your gentle approach is too careful
Misguided
Endearing
My fever boils over

Begging and wanting
Numb from the distant buzzing of heights
My mind feels so dizzy
In corners of cobwebs and rust

Your hand over mine in the shower
My thighs are on fire
Lusting your force and your power

Your tongue feels like Spring
My body grows weaker
Both watching each other for clues

Procrastination

I have to go
I cannot stay
I'll come again another day

Work must be done
And still I stay
I'll do the work another day

A list of things that wait their turn
Unattended, undisturbed
I've stared at them time and again

The list must wait
I'm too absorbed
To do the things
I have been told

The days go by
The dust builds up
The floors I would not eat off

The chores will wait
For I must stay
I'll do the tasks another day

Regret

Pretty soon we'll load the truck
Leave it all behind
Perhaps we're making a mistake
Too late to turn and run

Let's pack and leave
Start something new
Again
For what incentive do we go
What cause or motivation

Not sure what gain there is to find
Why can't we stay
No more regrets
Too late to wish for one more chance

Let's sit and think on this a while
Now, hurry up and go
Somebody's waiting for the key
So they can call this home

Speechless

You'd never think
Oh, joyous happy day
He stood to make a toast
Then fell
And there he lay

Wrong Side of the Glass

For those who wish to be disliked
Why should they try so hard
Their actions speaking louder than their words
Their message meaning less than nothing

You've got to ask yourself for what
Is there a purpose
Should there be one

Just then I spot a dying butt
Of a discarded shmig
The filter showing evidence
Of teeth and bright red lips

I am sitting opposite a couple
The girl is....
Who cares what she is wearing
I don't know anybody here

No one to understand me
They wouldn't try
They'd go away
Before they got too close

So, go away who needs you
The answer would be me
Still, if I ever got the chance
I wouldn't like them either

An Edited Excerpt from Tick Tock Tom

They were together. Yet, as the thought grew in his mind, he began to grow further and further apart from her. Soon, her presence no longer mattered.

All that mattered was this… thing… growing inside his head. His skull was beginning to show the strains of its girth.

Until now, the only way he was able to deal with his limitless existence was by not paying much attention to anything. This ability to defocus was what placed him in such high demand.

Over the years, it had allowed him to commit all sorts of atrocities. His conscience never had the chance to get the best of him. Not until now.

With no reason or explanation it was all coming back at him. They warned him that this day would come. But, why today?

Unsent Love Letter

I wrote my ex a letter and put it in a box
It was the closest I could come
To telling him my thoughts
My mind was overflowing
So what could be the harm
Of doing what I needed
In order to move on
So strange that I should miss him
More than when we were together
He was not the one
His friends had won the battle
I told him in my letter
He swore he knew a woman's place
That place which now sits empty
For me there's so much better
My heart a great big mess
I fight the urge to call him
With freedom now alone
Each day getting much harder
Each moment coming closer
To picking up the phone

Past Midnight

Touch me to make sure that I am here
Feel me to make sure that I am real
Be my only true concern

Here I float on air
With feet stuck in the clouds
Dangling upside down
Waving at the passengers of airplanes flying by

You always say it was a joke
You didn't really mean it
When you say so
I say no

You pretend that you were joking
A joke that does not want to end
The answer is still no
You seem to like rejection

You beg for me to put aside
All of my objections
All I can do is feel your lips
A simple kiss means nothing

Love

Forever less
Forever more
A loving touch
A tender kiss

No truer love to measure
Or ever feel alone
I know what torment feels like
You know where you can turn

The two of us can understand
The trust between two friends
So why not turn to me and say
I love you

Should We?

Here we are again
Deciding what to do
Afraid of stepping back
Afraid to get through

We go about our day
Hurting when we stumble
Our bearings disarrayed
Trying with futility not to lose our way

No Going Back

Why did we vest so much into each other
One day it will make sense
For now it does not matter

It's time for something new
Different
Hopefully better

Although our past was pretty good
Still we must bear our burdens
Before true happiness rings true

Your memories of me bear no regret
Cherish all we've done
Being better for the struggle

Hollow Wishes

Love me
Love me
Love me
Love me

For I love you

Is that it?

I guess so… no, it can't be

There must be more to it?
Nope, just love

Said as if it were so simple
After all this time

Full stop
Proving once again
One sided
Unfulfilled

Piece Two: Introspection

Cognac and Jasmine

I shouldn't have been drinking
I did it to myself
My throat is dry
I cannot sleep
Nobody else is up
I'm waiting now until the morning
Can't wait to start the day
A few more hours of this torment
Then I will leave my bed
I shouldn't have been drinking
I did it to myself

Mermaids' Song

If I had only listened
This would have been the way
I heard the Mermaids singing
Calling out your name

They would have told of yearning
To hold in cold embrace
Your quivering young body
Too tightly for your breath

No vapor would be wafting
From softly parted lips
No longer could you wander
Above the silver mist

I would have heard them whisper
To me, to all who'd hear
That time was passing quickly
Toward everlasting sleep

Free from the land and hardships
Complete without blood's game
Their arms were weaving tapestries
Through midnight stars and sky

The moonlight glistened timidly
Afraid to land too far
As I simply kept on walking
Their song a little high

If I had only listened
Perhaps I would have stopped
Perchance, I would have heard
Their lusting, soulful want

They are so unaccustomed
At being denied their prey
There isn't time to ponder
There isn't time to stray

I heard the Mermaids screeching
For, I had run to find
My love, my own life's partner
Before the sand ran dry

Aimless

My mind is dry
Thirst fills my dreams
I'm feeling uninspired

A void where words once freely flowed
Crisp, clean and full of purpose
Mountain streams of thought

Through mind to fingertips and keys
My muse brought chemistry with her
As a tornado trying to be caged

It hardly felt like work
Sparkling like magic and desire
Words sang and danced and played

For me, a humble servant
To her unyielding ways
Yet now I'm uninspired

Unsure where to begin
Attempting to keep going
The purpose now unseen

The Dove

Each day it came
Sat on my fence
Facing the wrong way

Sometimes alone
Sometimes with friends
Observing patiently

Then it would fly
Another perch
To check off for the day

I watched it sit
It's tail to me
One day the fence sat bare

Where had it gone
This bird of love
Why had it gone away

Some Guy on a Farm

Sitting here and typing
Hoping to be read
Something done at night
Everyone in bed

Some guy on a farm
Plowing his field
Sitting on a tractor
With PDA in hand

He's taking a break
From a hard morning's work
Checking what's being said
All around the World

That's where he has found me
Reading my two cents
If it has made him wonder
That was my intent

As Butterflies Dance

The sky is filled with warm crisp air
Refreshing and bewildering
Unknown to me what the day holds
Still new and waiting to unfold

Above my head a dance begins
Circling the clouds
Butterflies are fluttering
Each wing is full of purpose

The rustling of the leaves above
Removes me from my trance
Still nothing is so fully there
As these dancing butterflies

Surely they know what to do
What choices they must make
Undoubtedly there is a song
That answers all my woes

My eyes begin to fill the gaps
They glisten as they watch
The gentle gliding to and fro
Of insects and of foes

I blink and realize
Their daily dance is through
Its time to choreograph my own
My dreams to me are true

Understand Me

My grandmother is long since gone
I've tried so hard
Over the years
To make it all for something

For all these years I've always sworn
To write a simple novel
Of love and things she left behind
Her history
Her passion

Without the glue she used on us
Her absence still a void

I've tried so hard
Beyond her now
Her sacrifice and help

In weakness strength she did afford
So much unknown
So much unseen
So scared to live tomorrow

Breaking Away

Before you knew
Remorseful songs
Endearing words
Ardent embraces
Keenly you listened
Impatiently waiting
Needlessly pacing
Grasping for a turn

At last the moment had arrived
With little but a thought
A sudden jolt of motion took
Your life from house to rock

What Was Lost

For many years we tried and tried
At last we had a baby
We looked at her with marveling eyes
Her solitude inspiring

We tried again and didn't know
That prayers had been answered
Not knowing until far too late
What miracles dissolved

We'll never know who would have been
What heights he would have reached
He never got the chance to breathe

We'll never know
We'll never know
That's all he left behind

Sunrise

Tell me
Tell me
What is true?
For I know not this day
I blink
I cry
Fearing to die
And yet I must away

Passing Through

It does not feel like I belong
In this small place
With this small song

My days are fewer than before
They might run out
Leave only lore

Of things that I have left undone
My fill of youthful indiscretions
For fancy promises and lovers
Outstaying every welcome

No need to hang upon my wall
Mementos, photos, decorations
The next objective to surmount
Happily in sight

The others watch in disbelief
Some are still there
In each old place
For them, a final destination

My nerves are jumping at the chance
To prove them wrong I cannot stay
For fear my dreams desert me

The engine has been warm a while
Eagerly awaiting
For me to shift these restless gears
A transient state of boredom

Now What?

For years there was a dream to fill
Ambitious plans were made
Miraculous and simple things
Designed and then defined

Despite the finished timeline
Milestones ticked and checked
Indignant disbelief remains
At every finished task

Unwilling to accept my fate
Of happiness and glee
The things I wanted out of life
Belonging now to me

More than glass slippers have remained
No pumpkins rotting by the road
How can I trust this fragile state
From shattering like crystal

A Father's Love

Nobody except the trees
The sidewalk gloomy gray
The dark is all encompassing

With terrifying gaiety
Each rustling sound resounds
Leaves, air and everything
Collude to frighten me

Each sound assaults my senses
Basic natural fear
Unsure of my own mind
Oh, my! Is someone there?

Blissfully surprising
A soul wrapped in his gaze
Some fathers would not do the same
I run to his embrace

In Love We Repeat

I feel my hair drag in the breeze
As round and round we go
I saw that spot
It's there again
I'm happy now
You know
And still it's there
And there again
We've done all this before
I'd like to stop
When will this end
Yippee
And here we go

Rebirth

All your life you live as you
Then one day somebody new
Comes to live and share your home
Makes you feel like you're reborn
An exit wound unwraps your soul
So open now to full surrender
With each fresh day you seem to find
A new identity behind
The words and actions of your youth
That led you to this place on Earth

Three Steps to Nowhere

One day I lay awake in bed
Dreaming of shadows in my head
They passed from lobe to lobe to lobe
Memories that I had had no part in

It seemed to last a while before
He walked in through the open door
Not looking my way even once
Lying beside me
Turning twice

His back to me
My mind resumed
Wandering in lonely solitude

At risk of random acts of sin and meteoric impacts
How much does any of this matter
Floating about in open space
Vulnerable existence

We only live by pure coincidence
I bring it up a time or three
He shakes his head and simply says
"What do you want from me?"

Doubt and Loathing

I am not a good mo....
I am not a good wo....
I am not a good wi....
I am not a good pe....

I have a short fuse
I am lacking of sleep
I don't know how to love
Rage and doubt absorb me

I am desperate
I am disparate
I have nobody
I love nobody

If this were true
It would be
Of no consequence
I would sleep all night

I would not toss and turn
I would not have regrets
Do people ever have no doubts?
Does it even matter?

Did You Ever?

Did you ever want to pee
But didn't feel like going?

Did you ever tell yourself
That you would do it later?

Did you ever feel your eyelids drooping
As you lay thinking something up?

Did you ever wait for nothing
Not caring if it came?

Did you ever feel her crawling
Snuggling up behind you?

Did you ever feel her warmth surround you?
Did you ever love your life?

I want to start my day

The archetypal life direction was preset long ago
Some things had to take place in order
Based on what we know

First school
Then marriage
Then children

In between a life
A job
A love
A passion
The details weren't so clear

Somehow a lot of blanks laid bare
Directions all askew
It felt like something missing
A quest, a search unrealized

The point
What was the point
What is the point

In hindsight always present
In hindsight always there
The tough part is all over
Now to execute the plan

The ABCs of Captions

A quick synopsis of a thousand words
Astonishingly simplified
Amazingly concise

Bracing for a theory
Bragging of a deeper meaning
Brazenly aloof

Capitalized anticipation of images upheld
Commercialized redundancy
Cloaked in need to know

Shard Three: Life Lessons

Losing at Love

Alice loves to wonder
If he could be the one
He's handsome
Tall
Attentive

He leaves his clothes at rest
Discarded and disrobed
First rapturous then silent
All dressed and out the door

He doesn't call
She'll wait
She'll wait

After a month
No word
Move on

Alice likes to wonder
Perhaps this will be the one

Boy Parts

Boy parts are toy parts
Are fun, hard, and strong parts
Are nice, sweet, and small parts
Are parts that we simply can't do without

Girls doing boy parts can do them much better
Girls doing boy parts are stronger than ever
Girls can make boy parts and girl parts so clever

Cut up the fish parts and cook up the soup
Sing both the girl parts and boy parts together
Toss in some green and some red parts
Mix in some salt and some pepper to boot

We all set the table
The girls and the boys did
We all ate the dinner the boys had brought home

The boys sat together
Said they could do better
The boys can do better than say so and so

Girl parts are fun parts
Are soft parts
Are best not without parts

Girls like their boy parts
Boys need their girl parts
Neither is worth much all on their own

Dinosaurs

Nelson liked dinosaurs
She didn't care
Anything was good enough
If she could get his ear

She hung on every word he said
Dropped hints and clues galore
There was something about him
Something she adored

She tried each trick to get him
To strike a spark or two
But, Nelson just liked dinosaurs
Not her

Forest Stream

His name is forgotten
No longer the point now
Hair flowed behind him
In warm Autumn breeze

The twigs snapped beneath
Each step that he took
His eyes shone like topaz
A pulsating wolf

The stream ran alongside
The path where he tread
The camera snapped
Every move of his head

He told me a story
About the Prime Minister
Really about
The King Edward hotel

One day he got drunk
Went up to the penthouse
Demanded to know if Brian was there
He wasn't

A strange little joke
That walk in the forest
The stream that still flows there
The guy long since gone

Free of You

Sam, you're a maggot
Lice wouldn't bite you
That didn't stop me
I fell for your charm

You swore you'd protect me
Defend me
Respect me
You did no such thing
That's where I lay

It fell in three quarters
Each week a new setback
Then one day you stood there
Dumb luck as it were

My rose colored glasses
Suddenly missing
There standing before me
So grey and so dank

Your usual charm
Cloaked in stale smoke
Your money all spent on booze and on coke
Nothing for textbooks or gas to get home

Good riddance to you
Good bye and so long
The sex wasn't that good
I thought you should know

Love Forgotten

I left you in my rear view mirror
Glancing back not more than twice
You stood in shock and glared at me
Unsure if I'd turn back

The fight was odd
Out of the blue
Somewhat unprovoked

A simple word turned savage
Screams sharp as daggers heard
You weren't wrong and nor was I
In truth so long in coming

To say goodbye to one so loved
So dear
So beautifully gone

The rain started to pour harder
Difficult to see
The windshield wipers bent and swayed
Trying to keep pace

The car kept going
Foot firmly on the gas
Who could have known
A cut so clean was better

I Loved You in Silence

I used to sit and wonder
At couples who would meet
Inside of stylish restaurants
With working day complete

To sit unspeaking
Disconnected
Waiting for their food to come

I used to wonder
Why they did it
Why waste some much spare time

Then it was me who sat there
Waiting
Hoping
That you'll start the conversation going

For many years I sat there
Waiting
Hoping
Longing

I watched you sit in silence
Then we walked away
I loved you then in silence
I love you still today

He's Gone, Was It Worth It?

They sat at the dashboard
Staring out at the sky
He's a virgin he said
Let's try she replied

See if you like it
Her socks to her knees
Ankles put over her ears, if you please

That's all she was wearing
Beneath the moonlight
In front of the dashboard
On a dark starry night

Time rearranged initial direction
Of course he did like it
That's how things got started
But, half a year later no wedding assured

Each hotel got cheaper
The embers expired
As he asked the front desk
If they charged by the hour

Despite being expected
It still wasn't easy
When one day he'd moved on
To somebody new

Oh, Maryanne

Lick your wounds and dust your skirt
Brush your hair and smile
You know that time has been unkind
The years have passed you by

Chances that were never taken
Disasters left undone
No gains from ventures best unspoken
No milk stains on the floor

Children did not give you headaches
Or jump upon your couch
Now nobody will visit
Sunday dinners still for one

Your heart aches came only from watching
Soap operas and prime time
You stayed away from cads and liars
The backs of others being your guides

Today the sun rose over head
Birds chirped and trees have started blooming
The squirrels and birds have come and gone
The paper stays unread

Your coffee cup is empty
Your bank account still full
You're ready now to take a risk
But, who will risk on you?

Oxymoron

Antithesis
A commitment to an ideal
The feeling being that it is worth
An argument or two

Still it is not the point to make
Not worth the major title
It is a negative
Destructive

The antidote
The other side
The point behind the point

Removing from the goal
How can it be so minimal
So negligible
So dull

American Dollars

Lyudmila read the planets
Hasia read the cards
Fenya read the omens
Maria read the charts

The planets kept on shifting
They cards, they did not lie
The omens were all bad ones
Maria read the skies

The birds just kept on flying
The stars blinked in the night
Maria went on dreaming
The fish, they swam on by

The breeze, it swayed the curtains
The windows were ajar
The suitcases stood packed
The tickets in the car

Nobody came back there
The plans not realized
They caught her in the passage
Stopped from the tracks not far

Instead of a reunion
A memory remained
Instead of a new life
An old one laid to rest

Ruins of a Party

They sit and soak
All day and night
Hoping for somebody
To come and wash the dried on ruins
Of last night's celebration

Beside them lie
The silver tools
That aided in the doing
No more in glory and in shine
But with a lot of stuck on grime

The pots and bowls are not much cleaner
They wait their turn to come
And in the distance they lie thinking
That it is just their time

To go to bed
Leave till tomorrow
The toil and the distress
Of hands that have to scrub and rinse
These dishes in distress

Remnants of the Day

I like to hear about your day
What you did and where you stayed
It's nice to know who sat with you
How some small thing had made you blue

How warm the breeze
How cool the moon
The pictures that you drew

It's wonderful to see you smile
Watching you sleep
Dreaming of what you'll do tomorrow

What doesn't feel as good is this
The news we heard today
Some more got sick, a few more died
A car crashed through the crowd

I love to kiss your cheek
My arm beneath your head
Don't tell me anything tonight
Just stay with me and love me

Hunk Four: Commitment

Follow Along

A scratch
A sniff

A tug
A hug

Jump to the left
Jump to the right

A dance
A chance

A fluke
A look

Jump to the back
Jump to the front

Bend on over
Bend up right

The Honeymoon

Last night the weather was divine
A coverlet of shadow broken by the storm
Grey hair made humble by the rain
Draping like tapestries and cobwebs

Skin feeling damp beneath the coat
Nearby, the puddles rippled
Gusts of wind that know the way
To blow right through a person

A decade has gone by since then
The honeymoon less than romantic
Atmospheric pressure adding tension
What an approach to relaxation

On my left hand a ring
On my right side a husband
Venturing into the next chapter
Earshot away and deaf through the fog
Rapturous bouncing and sharing the news

In a new life the lesson learned
More caution and reserve
Would bring about a different end
Than one for which was yearned

Anticipation

We came and looked
We went away
At home we spoke
Decided

I went alone
We spoke some more
A little less divided

A day was somehow spent that way
It should have gone by faster
At home we looked and spoke some more

Move this one here and flip the door
The children let us do this
A simple change transforming minutes into days

Oh, well
It's done
So now we wait
We'll know by noon tomorrow

Will it be ours
Probably so
A house will be a home now

Never Apart

We're never apart
Always in sync
The hours pass slowly
Tick, tock
Knock, knock
Who's there?
What do you want?
The fear inside is here to stay
It never wanders far
There is no reason
No excuse
Irrational
Insane
Still all the time it nags
It gnaws
It won't let me alone
I'm scared
I'm terrified
It's there
The great unknown
Will you be here for me?

All I want is ....

Be careful what you wish for
No matter what you say
It could come back to bite you
The perfect wish astray

With pitch black sky there's time to think
When suddenly espied
A lonely twinkling star above
Wish I may and might

What should it be?
What do I want?
How dare I wish for something

All that I want
All that I need
Already in my grasp

Greed kills yet still I whisper
Hungry for some more
When suddenly a voice inside
Is shouting no, no, no

Snapping back from dreams insipid
I listen to it say
Be glad for what you have
Wish hard to keep it

Making Amends

Like a dog with tail between its legs
Walked in after another long day
Put down his bag
Washed his hands
Made dinner

It was payback
Retribution for the night before
After another long day
When all he wanted to do was to get away

He listened to everything she told him
He was involved and intimate
At night they sat and watched the rain
Too bad tomorrow the debt will have been paid

Besieged

My husband wants his wife back
He wants to have his supper
The house is much too dirty
The children must be fed
He wants her to stop dreaming
Stop trying and stop weaving
The delicately fragile
Silver web of hope
The end is not in sight yet
She seems so far away
Unwilling to return
Behind the ears still wet
How long will this obsession
Continue to possess her
When will he get his wife back
There's football on TV

Blood Thick Anger

The well of warmth and emptiness
Thick with blood-like stench
Grows dense with every moment
An onion cannot help

Tears will not come to cleanse
The hollow pit of anger
Complacent and unsure
Of how things came to pass

You never even knew me
You thought I was a whore
Reflected in my innocense
A motive of your own

The other day I saw you
The years have not been kind
Cluelessly still single
Your life still undefined

Your blindfold firmly planted
From where it will not lift
You still think I'm a whore
Despite a family of four

Husband

I'll tell you a tale of a peculiar beast
With nerves enough to spare
Sweat pouring down his shaven face
The man who wed one day

He did not bother to correct
The way I did in error
Bypass the candles to the side
To light the one in middle

I'll tell you of a mythic man
So wondrously perfect
Then I'll tell you of a lovely man
Who made me chicken soup

There are so many times
When I should keep my cool
So many moments when the mind
Can hardly grasp his logic

Who knows what many years will bring
If we will be together
There are some things that bind us now
Nothing bound us then

A million times we could have walked
That path we never chose
The day may come when we might part
For now, I do not want to

Splinter Five: Innocence To Crush Or Mold

Listen to me

Listen to me
Listen to me
Listen to me

Mama, mama, mama
Listen to me

Mama, mama, mama, mama
Listen I have something to say
I have to tell you a story

Okay, I say
What would you like to tell me?

Listen, mama, listen
I have something to say

Toddler Trot

He doesn't walk
He doesn't run
He briskly trots away

She simply watches as he goes
Along his merry way
He lingers here and there
For just a sec or two

His size, so small
Her wish, so tall
So much for him to do

The sun sinks lower still, tonight
Tomorrow's light unseen
What wasn't possible last week
Achieved with great esteem

Teacher's Day

An apple
A box of chocolates
A drawing
A card

What to bring
What to say
What to do
What to wear

Listen closely
Learn a lot
Remember all she's done

In we go
Meet and greet
Then out into the sun

Voices

The voices in my head
Surround and rise in volume
Constant chatter banging
Unwilling to abate

They won't shut up
Demanding my attention
Won't let me concentrate
Regardless of my pleas

There are some things that I must do
What do they care
They have their needs
Despite my obligations

I guess that I should listen
If only just to hear
This time belongs to them
One day they'll go away

Then I will want incessant droning
A distant memory
Of children playing while I work
Longing yet to come

Baking Cookies

The teacher marked the calendar
Everybody knew
Samuel would be five today
Small gesture and kind word

Asked mom to bake some cookies
For her to take to school
Franny spent all morning
Making all the food

She carefully distributed
To everyone's delight
The scrumptious little cookies
They savored every bite

Even teacher said so
But, Franny had her doubts
She was a little picky
Perhaps a tad bit shy

She wonders if they ate them
Just to spare her pride
What if they weren't good enough
She felt so odd inside

Growing Pains

Mary was too pretty
Sammy was too shy
Everybody wanted them
To come out and to try
They wouldn't budge
They wouldn't go
No matter what was said
But, then there are the evil ones
Caution justified
So Mary was too pretty
But, she learned how to fight
So Sammy was too shy
But, he learned how to shout

Perpetual Motion

The lion cub emits a roar
He fights with all his might
He won't sit still
He has to run
He has to build his score

Each cushion has a pin on it
Each stoop not good enough
From somewhere in a distant room
A sound comes wafting by

It makes him halt
Start spinning round
Then flying at full speed
He wants, he has to run and find
The source of so much glee

A blink or two and then he's off
No time to pause for long
So much to do
So much to see
A whirlwind on the ground

In Sickness

Yesterday she spent the day
Throwing up pure liquid
Helpless to do any good
I tried to be of service

Each heave painful to behold
Thankful for its passing
She leaned over the edge each time
No need for change of clothing

Yesterday I went to bed
Early and well beaten
Tough to tell if I was sick
Or tired of the sickness

The day before this all was fine
Today its chicken soup for breakfast
Tonight everybody's sleeping
Tomorrow might be my turn

Halloween Dread

My mind fills with dread
Cold sweat undead
Chilling embrace on my bones

What passed through my head
The children were fed
Desire for frolic and fright

The plans were all laid
Deep in the grave
Of ventures not yet undertaken

I cannot go back
My word holds me bound
By chains of immortal proportions

Unwilling to bow
Not inclined to indulge
My frightfully dizzying notion

That this Halloween
Must somehow surpass
The others that have come before him

Promise laid bare
Beholder beware
Abyss of dreadful devotion

To those little tots
Whose teeth candy rots
Beholden, truly beholden

Big Eyes Round World

I stay with great humility
That none should disagree
Her kisses are the best by far
In their simplicity

Each tear she sheds
Lead her astray
From mountains she must climb

Each fall, each drop
Cause her to bounce
Before the tears run dry

The urgent plea for one more hug
A testament, a swearing
Of oaths and bliss and honey bees
Her childhood and her glory

That face you make

You look at me
With accusation
How could I be so mean
Your eyes fill up with angry tears
Your face bright red and furrowed
The two front teeth that just broke through
Laid bare for all to see
Tears are pouring down your tiny face
Sleep fading from your eyes
Impatiently determined
Yet still unable
To tell me what you want

Frustration

Just when I think
That I am through
Beset by fresh demands

The way I thought that it would go
A forlorn fairy tale
Of ease and clarity

Why does it have to be so hard
When it should be so simple
To do this silly little thing

Sadness

Each time they leave
A pout appears
Screaming wait for me

I've got a gift to give to you
Don't leave
Not now
Not yet

Don't go
Why don't you stay tonight
I'll miss you when you're gone

With the door closed
She goes and plays
Licks at her wounds
And goes to bed

Another day
The door bell rings
She runs and jumps
They're here hooray, hooray

The Fifth Sense

There comes a time in every life
When all will abdicate
The right to point the way

The scale won't tip
Hindsight ahead
Heart and mind to trust

With senses as the only tools
Unsure of things once certain
Direction undefined

No light to shine or sound to guide
No object within reach
No one to answer what you ask

All you can do is trust
The way the scent describes to you
Which aura suites your plight

Sliver Six: The Sum and Its Parts

Tap, Tap, Tap

With a pat pat pat
And a tap tap tap
I love you sadly

With a hug hug hug
And a kiss kiss kiss
I love you gladly

With a pat pat pat
And a dab dab dab
I love you badly

With a clap clap clap
And a slip slap slop
I love you madly

Chipmunks and Ground Squirrels

So delicate and so determined
Always on the run
Busy day a little wilder
With every falling leaf

The chipmunk scurries
Runs
Oblivious to all who watch
Doesn't interact

It doesn't care for hand outs
Unlike the squirrel next door
So busy and without refrain
From taking human offerings

The other day a black one ran
Along the backyard fence
It had a tip of white
Capping off his tail

The skunk that lived beneath our porch
Had found a better dwelling
The squirrel decided to oblige
And move right in his place

A chipmunk would not be so eager
To use the recently vacated
The squirrel, an opportunist
The chipmunk, devoted and obtuse

The Shore

I love to sit
Watching the waves
Crashing on the shore

The only ones awake are me
The birds
The sky
The foam

The seashells lying scattered
Waiting to be found
I love to watch the ocean
Hear its peaceful sound

Energy

A distant erstwhile battle cry is heard
No simple undertaking
A bolt of lightning reaches through
Scratching the night sky

Each home that it caresses
Illuminates its darkness
Bright colors dancing wildly
A master and his muse

With thunder booming loudly
The torrent follows suit
It's heard in sweet November
Astounding lights and sounds

Through unexpected warmth
No snow upon the ground
Enveloping all those beneath
Awestruck and still unbound

Moonlight

Her hair hangs limply as she walks
Misty dew upon her shoulders
Dances on each blade of grass
Stars sparkling in the sky

She wraps her shawl around her waist
Hips swaying to the rhythm
Of strange sounds in the deep of night
Lips glistening with gloss

Her eyes are twinkling with delight
For all the things in life that glitter
A tiny giggle now escapes
At memories of old

Each folded tulip bowing forward
Each creature sleeping through the night
Even the owls have stopped their hooting
Even the nightingales slowed down

She steps beyond the fear of darkness
Bestowing sparkles on the ground
Believe in her, for she is moonlight
Elusive love that knows no bounds

Earth's Bones

Oh, Mother forgive me
I have been remiss
Your hair hangs so loosely
Your clothes all in tatters

My Lady
So gentle
So kind and so strong
Help me prepare thee
For things yet to come

I'm trying to rally
To bring back the sun
It shines far too brightly
The fish filled with poison
The waters all grime

Earth Mother hold me
The winds blow so strongly
I need to repent
Your trust disabuse

Oh, Lady of Plenty
Do not desert me
Forgive me
Bear with me
Stay with me a while

Hush

I have a secret for you
One you must never share
It is for you alone
That I lay down and bare
My most cherished deception
That deep within me lies
Some hidden talent
Some wonder to espy
Please keep it to yourself
Tell not a single soul
That I have nothing pressing
To keep you in desire
Your bated breath is wasted
For in me you will find
Only what you recognize
As what is yours to hide

Rocks & Stars

Collect them all
Scatter them about
The garden and the hearth

Sit back and watch
Learn how to love
To let them lie and die

Somehow they'll all outlast me
And you
And him
And her

Somehow they'll all still be here
Beneath this frozen Earth
Harboring no ill will
To those that left them thus

Energy and mass
Waiting to be challenge
Ignited and delivered
With dignity and class

Quest for Satisfaction

You have to wonder why you try
Crying at the sweat
From thoughts and dreams and wishful thinking
Cluttering your head

Buzzing sounds of things undone
Perhaps even unsaid
So many years that used to be
Ahead of nipping youngsters

Through blood and tears
Through shear determination
At crossroads in the middle

You could be faster, better, smarter
You could be richer, bigger, fatter
You could be worse
Regret a pointless feeling

Though there were times you were convinced
That failure overshadowed
Looking back it seems so clear
All roads would always lead you here

Each thing you did and moment passed
Bemused and full of awe
All you can do is what you've done
That's all that you can ask for

A Dream Realized

Inspiration curdling
Alive and somehow dead
My spirit is alright
My tongue is mute instead

Derived from heart to mind
From soul to motivation
Planned many years before
Somehow always implicit

Commenced on realization
That planning out your dreams
Is different
From living them

Broken Axle Spinning Blind

I'll make no excuses
It is what it is
The needle lays wasted
A torrent of woes

The axle spins blindly
Foretold and forsaken
Beneath skies of blue
Above the burnt umber

The doodles were carvings
Of life's grander pastures
Pregnant with wanting
Just out of reach

That which surrounds me
The clues to a riddle
Enigma unraveled
Through hindsight and fate

A Soul Laid Bare

I did it
I did it
It's good

Lay open your mind
And then judge me
Perhaps there is something to gain

Lay open your heart
But be wary
Perchance who you judge is yourself

Missing the Bus

The bus comes every day
At roughly even time
There must be some demand for it
Or else it would not come

To take those to and from
Where they might hesitate
It gets the ones who wait
To get on with their day

Sometimes it would be nice
To know when it is due
To hop aboard and go
To places I abhor

Then I look up to see
I've missed it once again
Admonished by no one but me
Then happy once again

Afterword

Secret Passage

The title *Broken Axle Spinning Blind* was selected for its symbolic reference to the displacement experienced on transition from one stage of life to another. Each new chapter is often welcomed by a mixture of emotions. It is only natural to find ourselves going through some sort of introspection. Re-evaluating lessons learned, commitments, responsibilities, and needing to justify where we had been and where we are going.

Embarkment on new phases is often accompanied by what feel like shards, hunks, splinters, slivers, fragments, and pieces of experiences that leave the aftertaste of having been victimized by life and all humanity.

The poetry within is an exploration of these stages of life and a coming to terms with the similarities and differences that bind us all. When royal houses began to fall as a result of too much in-breeding, people started to realize that diversity is important. The idea of purity seemed more natural, until they realized that nature depends on imperfection. Still, danger lies when dwelling too long on disjointedness.

Life has only one purpose, and that is to exist. Each object and organism has a part to play in the bigger picture, and in this way is only a part of a greater whole. However, no one part can contribute fully without being entirely self-absorbed with its own survival.

In this sense, even that which is without the ability to function on an intellectual level interacts, aids, and impedes the flow of the greater good. Of course, these are ridiculous notions since something within itself cannot impede something outside of itself, if it is entirely contained. Therein lies the human condition.

Looking strictly at human-to-human interaction, there are two macro groups of concern: Gender and Culture. Each is a subgroup of the other and both in harmony and at odds within every possible combination.

There is internal and external friction which will never be resolved because life cannot exist without unrest. Instead there is a cyclical struggle to establish and regain equilibrium. Existence is not possible without a reasonable amount of elasticity.

To this end, it is impossible to fully realize individual goals without inconveniencing others. Ultimately, this is as much essential and good as it is imperative to negate. There cannot be an up without a down and it is impossible to remain in either position indefinitely.

This is the ultimate song and dance, and at its heart there is a rhythm. There must be a winner and loser in any battle worth waging. What's more, one side is often slightly more committed to the fight than the other.

While there may be sense in discussing concepts such as survival of the fittest, we cannot assume that the scale by which fitness is judged is based on common goals. Here, too, there is no consensus. It can be argued that the simplest organism is the strongest since it wants for nothing and needs nothing to exist.

Similarily, the human being could be said to be the weakest life form because it cannot live without food, shelter, and companionship of others. The ability to reason is compensation for a complete inability to survive without it. In this sense, all of nature is superior to us, who believe that we are the most significant of all of G-d's creations. Perhaps the ability to reason was only given to us as a last resort, as a means of giving us a fighting chance.

We contemplate our own existence and debate right from wrong as a natural consequence and balancing mechanism against the ability to determine that there is no reason to get up in the morning if all there is to life is procreation and death. It could be said that there is no point to all our struggles if existence itself is temporary. The drive to leave a mark is a bit comical considering how closely our specific existence and legacy is tied to a planet that has already begun to die.

Without the ability to debate the validity of such ideas we would be defeating life's ultimate purpose. Consider that we have less than a fraction of the information of what our greater whole really entails. So, it is impossible to definitely prove if we are even asking the right questions, let alone finding the right answers.

There really is no way to know for certain what impact our entire planet has on all that of which it is only a tiny element. All we can know is what we are given access to and what we think that means.

On this, there is no agreement, either. So, there is struggle. Ultimately, one side becomes temporarily dominant, while the other is religated to victim status.

By definition, a victim is a person for whom a bargain is unfair. The cost extracted is not worth what is delivered in return. Some are made into victims, some do it to themselves, and some are born that way. What matters is not how a person or group becomes victimized, only what they choose to do about it.

There is a long-standing debate on if there is such a thing as free-will. Let's assume that there both is and is not. We must agree that life, in general terms, is driven by something outside of individual preference. Point one for no free-will. But, divine creation is not concerned with the micro-management of existence, only that there is existence. In this sense there is free-will, and an obligation to assert it.

The only choice is which side to lie down with. If fairy tales are life lessons not necessarily for the young, then there is no better place to look for guidance. These stories have been passed down through the ages and modified by many. Thanks to the efforts of the Brothers Grim and Walt Disney, children are not the only people who now know little of the more raw and telling versions of tales like Sleeping Beauty, and Cinderella.

After all, life was different before technology. It was harsher, more brutal. There were different ethics. Different views of women. Different lessons to be learned.

There were no televisions, and therefore no soap operas. Long before Romans attended Coliseums to determine if men lived or died with thumbs up or down, people lived up in remote villages and still needed to be thrilled and entertained on a long, cold winter nights.

A gentle kiss to wake a sleeping virgin was not enough. What's more, people had far less patience with delicate, privileged creatures. For them, the fun was in hearing of horrible things happening to those that did not have to work as hard as they did, and who reaped rewards off the backs of others.

It is little wonder that most of the fairy tales of old were less than suitable bed-time reading material. In their original forms, Cinderella, Sleeping Beauty, Rumpelstiltskin, Rapunzel, and Little Red Riding Hood, all had a good dose of some combination of deceit, mutilation, cannibalism, brutality, rape, and even seduction of grown men and beasts by prepubescent girls. There were few happy endings and even fewer happy in-betweens.

In most of the stories the girls are either abandoned or orphaned by their parents and forced to endure unspeakable abuses at the hands of those charged with their care. There is usually a prince or a king of some sort but, this is a man whose first interaction with the girl would be of a less than noble sort.

The earliest versions of Cinderella had the prince looking for the girl's fur slipper rather than a glass one. Sleeping Beauty and Snow White both got impregnated and gave birth to twins prior to waking up.

Many earlier versions also saw a great number of infant casualties. The baby that Rumpelstiltskin worked so hard for didn't fare any better than Sleeping Beauty's illegitimate offspring.

The Little Mermaid is a victim of a different sort. Yes, her mother died when she was young. However, she had a loving father, aunt, and older sisters who all cared deeply for her. She was a princess of an undersea kingdom. She was safe and had no demands placed on her, short of staying away from the water's surface until she came of age.

The choices that she made were driven by her own curiosity and desires. In striking a bargain with the Sea Witch, she embarked on a downward spiral of events without being coerced by anybody. She entered into the contract knowing of the possibility of failure and risking everything for love.

While Disney would have you believe that the prince's heart is tied to the debt he feels for the girl that saved him. In the original tale, we discover that there is a separation of motives. In fact, while it may have been his initial motivation, we learn that he has had time to get to know both the little mermaid, in her silent human form, and the girl from the convent that later found him. He had time to decide whom he really wanted, and the mermaid knew that it was not her.

This is not to say that Shakespearean justice was not served on the villains, as well. The Wicked Queen from Snow White rolled down a hill in a barrel full of nails pointing inward; Cinderella's stepsisters cut off their toes and heals trying to fit into the slipper, and had their eyes pecked out by birds; and depending on whom you ask, Rumpelstiltskin was so upset at getting outsmarted that he either stomped himself into the ground and then got torn in half while being pulled out, or got torn in half as the guards tried to extricate him from the Queen, into whom he had launched himself.

Each of the tales, and those hundreds not mentioned, all speak of victims of humanity's cruelest tendencies. In many, the girls had little choice in their circumstances. If they were not born with a predetermined fate, it was thrust upon them.

One could argue that very early versions of a seven year old Little Red Riding Hood doing a strip-tease to distract the wolf depict the innate wanton lust of women and further the notion that all women are whores. Even with Sleeping Beauty and Snow White, the girls are raped and impregnated and on waking are said to live happily ever after with their perpetrators.

Let us not forget that these stories were written by men. In those times, and still today, many men do not see rape as anything other than what a woman deserves and desires. After all, it is a well known fact that when a woman says no, she really means yes. So, since rape is not really a bad thing, and women are not people then, both are no more than literary tools used to entertain, educate, and further the story.

The audience was never meant to get emotionally vested in the victims' initial plight, returning us once again to the notion of individual choice. The choice is not about the atrocities that befall us. Rather it is about how carnage and mayhem are received by the participants.

Rapunzel's father is forced to strike a bargain with the old woman. On the one hand, he is forced to steal to appease his wife's cravings. On the other, he is forced to pay for his indiscretion.

Back in his day, it was unthinkable to deny a woman her craving, and his wife is no more to blame because she is not considered responsible for her hunger. The old woman cannot be blamed, either. Not because she begrudged a sprig of parsley, or rapunzel, or even cabbage. After all, the first two are basically edible weeds and the second was always considered to be poor man's food. No, her problem was her solitude and desire for companionship.

So, since we can feel for each of the founding characters, the villain must be the new-comer to the story: The young girl. Not only has she not proven any need for us to feel sorry for her but, she is young and beautiful. To this day, there are few things as enticing as hearing tales of bad things happening to beautiful people, at least initially.

The girl's parents become of no consequence and we never learn if they are left childless or end up having more. Likely they had more, and in any case, a girl wasn't worth much back then, so it couldn't have been a big loss. They are the forgettable victims, left without their daughter, and without our interest in what happens to them.

By contrast, as Rapunzel hits puberty she is locked away. She is robbed of all freedom and persecuted for doing what was humanly natural. Unlike her father, who took the raw deal, she fought back, unwilling to accept the fate the old woman had designed for her. She sought out her prince and despite his disfigurement was able to save him.

Cinderella, too, though beaten down over many years and in every way possible, does not allow her spirit to get broken. In a final moment of weakness she gets a little ghostly or magical assistance. However, it is her inner strength which permits her to take advantage of sudden opportunity, and is the ultimate deciding factor of her fate.

We all know people who accept what is given to them. They permit others to dictate and obey the will of those who mean them harm. Those are the people that victimize themselves. True strength lies with those who refuse to be victims despite being victimized.

The Little Mermaid was filled with all sorts of rebellion and capacity for youthful indiscretion. No matter what she did, her family remained her enablers. She was the essence of a truly spoiled child.

There were no hidden clauses in her contract with the witch. No promises or tricks to justify our empathy. She was made aware of what her actions may lead to but, never appreciated the risk, since she was never denied anything.

It is a heartbreakingly tragic coming-of-age story where the heroine makes the ultimate sacrifice. She surrenders more than her own chance at happiness. She gives up her immortality and relinquishes her soul's ability to survive her.

Through true love and surrender she is vindicated and redeemed. Her final forfeit speaks of true selflessness and love. Once she refuses to play victim to her own vanity she is forgiven and re-gifted her soul. In truth, the moral is inspirational and gratifying.

Fairy tales of old are rarely about cultural conflicts. Instead, they focus on internal issues and use their cultural biases as the backdrop and justification for which side to put forth as the heros and which to label villains. If there are lessons to be learned, they are taught based on the ethics and morals of the society in which they are told.

For this reason, there are so many variations that span both continents and generations. The Egyptian Cinderella is not at all the housekeeper of France. Her sisters are not a couple of spoiled sisters. Instead, they are fellow harems dwellers. Girls bought and sold as property and forced to compete for the affections of kings through the only thing at their disposal; their sensuality.

Behind all this belies the point that all life and humanity cannot exist without struggle. Just as a child cannot be born without conception, pregnancy, and labor. All of humanity depends on the ability to victimize and rebound, to be downtrodden and then rise above.

About The Author

Born in 1973, Freyda Tartak emigrated from Europe to Canada in the early 1980s. Since then, she has been living in the suburbs of Toronto, Canada and has traveled extensively throughout North America and Europe.

Freyda has published numerous articles on a wide range of topics, with work appearing online, as well as in various newspapers and magazines.

Despite rarely having a spare moment, there are few things Ms. Tartak relishes more than sitting on the front porch with her husband, a warm cup of tea, and a thunderstorm.

www.ingramcontent.com/pod-product-compliance
Lightning Source LLC
Chambersburg PA
CBHW031401040426
42444CB00005B/379